Avoid being in a Medieval Castle

Written by
Jacqueline Morley

Illustrated by
David Antram

Created and designed by
David Salariya

The Danger Zone

BOOK HOUSE

Contents

Author:
Jacqueline Morley studied English at
Oxford University. She has taught English and
History, and now works as a freelance writer.
She has written historical fiction and non-fiction
for children.

Artist:
David Antram was born in Brighton, England,
in 1958. He studied at Eastbourne College of Art
and then worked in advertising for fifteen years
before becoming a full-time artist. He has
illustrated many children's non-fiction books.

Series creator:
David Salariya was born in Dundee, Scotland.
He has illustrated a wide range of books and has
created and designed many new series for
publishers in the UK and overseas. He established
The Salariya Book Company in 1989. He lives in
Brighton with his wife, illustrator Shirley Willis,
and their son Jonathan.

Editor: **Stephen Haynes**

Editorial Assistants: **Mark Williams,
Tanya Kant**

Visit our website at **www.salariya.com**
for **free** electronic versions of:
You Wouldn't Want to be an Egyptian Mummy!
You Wouldn't Want to be a Roman Gladiator!
Avoid Joining Shackleton's Polar Expedition!
Avoid Sailing on a 19th-Century Whaling Ship!

Published in Great Britain in 2008 by
Book House, an imprint of
The Salariya Book Company Ltd
25 Marlborough Place, Brighton BN1 1UB
www.salariya.com
www.book-house.co.uk

HB ISBN-13: 978-1-906370-25-1
PB ISBN-13: 978-1-906370-26-8

SALARIYA

3 5 7 9 8 6 4 2

A CIP catalogue record for this book is available
from the British Library.

PAPER FROM
SUSTAINABLE
FORESTS

Printed and bound in China.
Printed on paper from sustainable sources.
Reprinted in 2011.

Introduction

You're a country girl in 13th-century England. You're used to a farming life, so you really think you're in luck when you get the chance to work in the local castle. You imagine you'll be mingling with lords and ladies – the sort of grand people who speak French to each other!

But there's trouble ahead. The year is 1215 and King John is in a power struggle with his barons. They're lords of Norman-French descent who have been the ruling class in England since the Normans conquered it, a century and a half ago.

The king has been forced to sign an agreement with the barons – the Magna Carta or Great Charter – which gives them the right to overrule the king. But John shows no sign of sticking to the agreement. When some of the angry barons rebel, you find yourself caught up in a terrible siege.

The ruins of Rochester castle, Kent, as they are today. This book is based on the true story of the siege of Rochester castle in 1215.

The castle across the river

You're helping with the harvest but you're dreaming of the castle. You'll be living there soon! Your father has got you a job there. These villeins (peasant farmers) don't like your father. As bailiff of the castle estate, his job is to see that they work as hard as possible for the lord of the castle.

THE BAILIFF makes the villeins work the lord's land, in return for the right to use some of the land for themselves.

HE DEALS with the reeve (the spokesman for the villeins) and the hayward (who mends fences and rounds up strays).

Perhaps I'll have a lovely room with a view of the river...

MUCH of the villeins' own harvest goes to the lord as rent. This poor woman is paying her rent in eggs – only the rich use money.

MOST VILLEIN HOMES have just two rooms; one of them is for the animals. Your father's house is much grander – it has three rooms!

Handy hint

Five men can harvest two acres (0.8 hectare) in a day, as every bailiff knows. Don't let them take longer – they're just being lazy.

Rochester castle

Rochester cathedral

Why would they want **her** in the castle?

I suppose she thinks she's better than us.

In the bailey

I t's the great day! You've come with your father to the castle. When you pass through its gate into the bailey – that's the area inside the castle walls – you're amazed to find that it's just like a busy village inside. There are stables, barracks, and all sorts of other wooden buildings around the walls. Everything you need to live on is here. There's a small farm with vegetable plots, cow sheds, a poultry yard and a dairy. In the big central space, men-at-arms are being drilled.

WHILE YOUR father talks with the marshal (he's head of military supplies), you watch the farrier shoeing a huge warhorse. 'A warhorse is the most expensive thing a knight has to buy,' he tells you.

So... What's your excuse?

Gatehouse

I thought this was a friendly match!

MEN-AT-ARMS (soldiers who are not knights) wrestle to keep fit while they're not on guard duty. When a lord needs warriors he summons knights from their estates.

THESE VILLEINS are accused of grinding their corn at home instead of paying to have it ground at the lord's mill. They'll be tried by the sheriff at his court in the castle.

Key to the bailey:

(Note: The wooden buildings have not survived – we can only guess what they were like.)

1 Barracks
2 Armoury
3 Smithy
4 Stables
5 Kennels
6 Almonry
7 Storage barn
8 Chapel and belfry
9 Guesthouse
10 Hall and buttery
11 Kitchen
12 Bakehouse
13 Brewhouse
14 Laundry
15 Dispensary
16 Chandlery
17 Poultry yard
18 Cattle shed
19 Dairy
20 Hay barn
21 Tool and wagon shed

Handy hint

A well-stocked bailey is no use if attackers can get in. Protect it with a strong gatehouse and a drawbridge over a moat.

Keep

Exercise yard

Kitchen garden

Cattle yard

Orchard

Outer wall or curtain wall

The Keep

'Haven't I seen you here before?'

Archbishop's private apartments

Archbishop's private chapel

Furniture under wraps

Trestle table packed away

Archbishop's state rooms

Sheriff's court in the Great Hall

Storage rooms at ground level

A cutaway view of the castle keep.

Will I be seeing the lord of the castle?' you ask nervously when you reach the keep. Your father laughs. 'No, he's much too grand. He's the Lord Archbishop of Canterbury – the most important churchman in the country. He's hardly ever here. The castle is run by his deputy, the Constable. He's an important baron and you will be serving his wife.'

Your new job

YOUR FATHER leaves you with the chamberlain, a busy man in charge of household affairs. He takes you to the Great Chamber where the ladies spend the day. The Constable's wife lives like a great lady, with damsels (ladies-in-waiting) to wait on her. One of the older ladies explains your duties. Clearly she doesn't think much of you. 'You need new clothes,' she says. 'We don't want ragamuffins. You'll get some as Christmas pay. Till then you'll wear cast-offs.'

If attackers ever break into the bailey, the castle dwellers can shut themselves safe and snug inside the keep. Its walls are thick, its windows small and high, and its entry well protected. Its cellars are stocked with food and weapons, and it has its own well. The first floor, where the Constable lives, is split by a wall into two large rooms: the Hall, where he conducts business, and the Great Chamber for family use. The Archbishop's rooms above are under wraps until he comes.

Handy hint

Medieval advice to an untrained servant: 'Do not claw your back as if you were after a flea, or stroke your hair as if you sought a louse.'

And stand up straight when I'm talking to you!

I want to go home.

She was just the same when I started working here.

A castle day

At noon everyone eats in the hall in the bailey. The Constable, his lady and the household officials sit at the 'high table' at the top end of the hall. Everybody else sits at trestle tables down the length of the hall, with the more important people nearer the top. You're right at the bottom, next to a smug-looking page. He helps himself to stew, spooning it onto the trencher of bread in front of him. You copy him, so he'll think you know how to behave. Then he starts talking French – just to embarrass you!

Bonjour.

How many robes has she got?

COCKCROW. Horror! Last night you forgot to get water for the ladies' morning wash. You sneak to the indoor well in the hall while the men are still putting away their beds – strictly forbidden!

NEXT you help the ladies dress. You liven up the fire and warm their clothes in front of it. You help them pull on their hose (stockings) and hold the mirror while they do their hair.

YOU PUT the daytime cover on her ladyship's bed, tie back its curtains and put away the maids' truckle beds. Then you go to Mass, which everyone attends in the bailey chapel.

THE ELDERLY, sour-tempered damsel takes you to the wardrobe, a room where clothes are stored. Here you spend the morning cleaning fur-lined robes by rubbing them with bran.

IN THE AFTERNOON the ladies hunt with falcons. The Constable's Lady keeps hers in the Great Chamber. You have to sweep up its droppings and put clean rushes on the floor.

EVERY SPARE moment must be spent spinning – twisting wool into thread. When the ladies return, you are beaten with your own distaff for letting the dog foul the rushes.

THE LADY has a bath quite often – once a month or so – in a big half-barrel which is lined with cloth in case of splinters. You have to keep topping it up with hot water.

YOU SLEEP on a straw pallet at the draughtier end of the room. From where you lie there's a strong whiff from the garderobe (toilet). It's worse than your outdoor privy at home.

From page to Knight

EVERY PAGE hopes to become a squire – and every squire hopes to become a knight.

THE NIGHT before the knighting ceremony, the squire takes a bath and dresses in white to symbolise his purity of spirit.

HE SPENDS all night praying in the chapel. Next morning he makes his confession to the priest and hears Mass.

THE PRIEST blesses the squire's sword. The lord then 'dubs' him knight by striking him on the shoulder with this same sword.

That smug page is so full of himself, you could kick him.

'My father is a baron and lives in a castle,' he tells you, 'so of course he's sent me away from home to get a good tough education. I've lived here since I was seven. I'm learning to be a knight, and when I'm fourteen they'll make me a squire like my brother. He is squire to the Constable. He serves him at table, looks after his horse and arms, and rides with him into battle. One day he'll be a knight.'

You've seen the page training in the bailey, and you think you'd make a much better squire than him. When he rode at the quintain he was much too slow and the weight swung round and hit him.

Did you ever see anything like it?

AFTER A FINAL blessing everyone celebrates. These ceremonies are not essential. A lord can reward a brave man by dubbing him knight in the thick of battle.

IN PEACETIME, knights hold practice fights called mêlées. There are no rules – they just attack each other, and some get killed.

Clannng!

Handy hint

A squire should keep his knight's armour sparkling by rolling it in a barrel of sand, then polishing it with a wad of horsetail plant.

Thwack!

Knight in shining armour? Damsel in distress, more like!

The quintain is a swivelling target mounted on a post. It's used to practise charging with a lance.

The sandbag adds weight to the target, so you have to hit it pretty hard. Then you're supposed to get out of the way before the bag swings round.

The Lord comes to stay

The Lord Archbishop is on his way! Everyone is in a rush, sorting out stabling, rooms and food for the huge household of officials and servants he'll be bringing with him. Great lords always travel like this. They have several homes and move from one to another. If they stayed put, their household would soon exhaust the local food supply. So they move on, taking their possessions with them. The archbishop brings his clothes, knock-down furniture, state hangings, bed covers, household linen, chapel furnishings, buttery and kitchen equipment, church candles and barrels of best French wine.

Fit for a lord?

THE ARCHBISHOP'S officials arrive some days ahead to see that his rooms are in order. Does the chimney still smoke; do the shutters fit; are the hangings up?

That won't do!

HIS STEWARD insists that the Archbishop's chamber needs whitewashing, and there must be a better chest for displaying his gold dishes when they arrive.

HIS BAKER comes to make the Archbishop's favourite French bread. He's far too grand to cook it himself, of course – he gives orders to the castle staff.

Handy hint

Be prepared for a big crowd at the almonry, where charity is given to the poor. When there's a banquet, beggars flock from far and wide.

IN HIS STATE CHAMBER, the Archbishop is holding a banquet for local nobles. The walls are hung with painted cloths and a state canopy hangs over his throne. The high table is elegantly draped and set with gold plates. Trumpeters herald each course and his carver kneels before him, waiting to serve. Musicians play in the gallery.

Rebel barons

LONDONERS are backing the rebels at the moment – but if John returns with a foreign army they may be forced to change their minds.

THE CONSTABLE welcomes the barons.

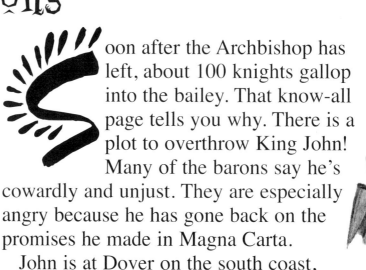

Soon after the Archbishop has left, about 100 knights gallop into the bailey. That know-all page tells you why. There is a plot to overthrow King John! Many of the barons say he's cowardly and unjust. They are especially angry because he has gone back on the promises he made in Magna Carta.

John is at Dover on the south coast, waiting for foreign help. Rochester castle controls the route from Dover to London, so the Archbishop is letting the barons take over the castle to stop the King returning to the capital.

Squawk!

Er... that's it!

BUT THE CASTLE is not ready for more visitors so soon after the Archbishop's visit! There are hardly any weapons in the armoury.

Plip!

THERE'S NOT much food or wine in the cellars, either. Entertaining the Archbishop has used up all the reserves.

THE REBELS raid the city of Rochester, forcing terrified citizens to part with their supplies at swordpoint.

Make yourselves at home, lads!

Handy hint

Ever fancied being a messenger? You get good wages and a free horse, but be prepared to ride hard, day or night.

This could be fun...

The cowardly, unjust King is coming!

This could be dangerous...

A MESSENGER gallops in to warn the rebels that the King is on his way with a huge army to attack the castle.

The bridge

The rebels know they'll be outnumbered, but they're not going to surrender. They're sure the barons in London will soon send help. Till then they must prepare for a siege, so the Constable has ordered everyone on the castle's estate to bring in food at once. You've been sent home to fetch whatever your family can spare. Returning to the castle, you are horrified to find that the King's men are already there, in boats, setting fire to the struts of the bridge!

River Medway

What is a siege?

The idea of a siege is to surround the castle with troops so that the defenders cannot get out, or bring supplies into the castle. Once they have run out of food, they will have to surrender. Destroying the bridge will cut the castle off from the west.

I hope we can get back in.

THE BOATS have been beaten off, but your heart is in your mouth. Will the bridge still support the cart, the cow and you?

Creak!

SOON THE attackers are back in greater numbers. They destroy the bridge and take over the city.

I hope we can't.

Handy hint

In a siege, you need a water supply that the enemy can't cut off. Otherwise you may have to drink urine or horse's blood.

KING JOHN uses the cathedral as a stable for his horses. The clergy are horrified.

SAFELY BACK in the castle, you see that the hill overlooking the bailey is covered with tents and armed men. Will you be safe for long?

Casualties

he siege is in its second week now. Scared and exhausted, you're in the keep, digging crossbow bolts out of men's flesh and binding their wounds. There are a thousand of the King's men outside, firing crossbows at the defenders on the outer walls and trying to put up scaling ladders.

Worse still, five mighty trebuchets are hurling rocks into the bailey, smashing its wooden buildings to bits and pounding the stone walls.

A TREBUCHET works like a see-saw. A huge boulder is placed in the sling. Then the sling arm is pulled down with a winch. When the arm is let go, the massive weight on the other end makes it shoot up again, hurling the boulder into the air.

Sling

Sling arm

Trebuchet

Winch

Weight (box of boulders)

The wall's down!

They're getting into the bailey!

A CONSTANT RAIN of boulders on one part of the wall produces first a crack, then a crumbling, then collapse.

Don't worry about him, dear. At least he's still well enough to scream.

Handy hint

Spiral stairs must turn clockwise. That gives you elbow-room (if you're right-handed) to swing your sword against an attacker climbing up towards you.

YOU THROW a firepot yourself, just to show that useless page, struggling with his crossbow, that you can fight too.

HE'S YANKED the bowstring into place at last! He takes aim at someone who looks very like the King. But a rebel knight reminds him that it would be a sin to kill an anointed king – even a bad one.

Oh... yes... I suppose so.

Urgh!

Pant!

DEFENDERS on the roof of the keep are calling for firepots (pottery bombs filled with tar and lighted rags) to drop on the enemy below.

23

The tower collapses

It's week five of the siege. Everybody who escaped death when the bailey fell has fled to the keep. Conditions here are dreadful. People are crowded in, with barely room to lie down to sleep, and very soon the food will run out. The trebuchets are still pounding, though surely they can't make much of a dent in the walls of the keep – they are nearly 4 metres thick. The enemy's ladders are useless too: the keep is much too high to scale. Perhaps you can hold out until help arrives from London – or perhaps not...

Ooh-er!

ONE DAY, while dressing wounds in the south tower of the keep, you notice that the surface of the water in a storage jar is quivering. What could be making the tower vibrate? You decide to raise the alarm.

THE TOWER is being mined! The King's men are digging a tunnel underneath the base of the tower. Its timber roof is held up by wooden props.

Archers protected by wooden shelters called hourdes or hoardings.

Arrow slit

Baskets of earth

Wooden shelter covered with animal hides

Pit props

Talus (stone ramp to protect base of wall)

THE MINERS carry props in and take earth out under a protective shelter.

Mine

24

THE MINERS
make a deep
cavity under the
tower and pack it
with brushwood.

Handy hint

Miners beware!
Defenders will try to
drop firepots on your
shelter. Cover it
with hides and
keep them
wet.

*King John has
sent for 40 pigs.*

Oink!

THE KING'S MEN use pig fat
to start the brushwood burning.
When the props burn through,
the tunnel ceiling collapses, the
ground subsides and the
tower falls.

RUMBLE!

CRASH!

This way, lads!
We've got them
cornered now!

Holding out in the Keep

A quarter of the keep has crashed to the ground. The King's men have poured into the Great Chamber but they cannot get control of the whole keep. The rebels have barred the connecting doors between the Chamber and the Hall and are fighting on from there. They have almost no food left, and nothing to drink but water – a liquid that's considered fit only to wash in. You are simmering a few scraps of horsemeat when you see the door leading to the floor above begin to open. John's men are trying to get in from upstairs! The guard is too quick for them this time, but how much longer can the rebels hold out?

If you can't fight, you can't eat!

...that's what I heard!

The swine!

THERE'S NOT enough food to go round, so the rebels force everyone who cannot fight to leave – even though they are bound to be captured by the enemy.

YOU DON'T WANT to be flung to the enemy so you hide as best you can. By the time you're noticed, no-one has time to bother with you.

YOU HEAR what happened to the ones who did go: John had their hands and feet cut off!

Goodbye to the castle

KING JOHN is thinking of celebrating his victory by having every one of the rebels hanged.

Starvation finally forces the rebels to surrender, after nearly two months of bitter siege. By this time you hardly care what happens; the enemy will kill you if the hunger doesn't. Luckily you are far too lowly for anyone to bother with you. Even the rebels are spared by the King's greed and cowardice; he's afraid that if he punishes the barons now, they'll get their own back later. He seizes the castle and staffs it with people loyal to himself.

Nobody messes with me!

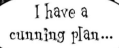

I have a cunning plan...

Don't you worry about them, my girl – serves the blighters right!

BUT A FOREIGN captain has a better idea: the King should give each of his cronies a rebel to hold for ransom (keeping the most valuable for himself, of course).

THE KING still wants a bit of fun, so he hangs just one crossbowman, on grounds of ingratitude: the man had been raised in the royal household, so he ought to have been loyal.

Pig fat! They used pig fat!

Now your father is no longer bailiff and you're back home working on the land. You feel sorry for that wretched line of rebels being led off to moulder in castle prisons for who knows how long. What a joy to think you need never set foot in a castle again!

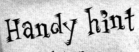

Handy hint

Don't let an important captive go too cheaply. The longer you hold on to him, the more his family may be willing to fork out for him.

What came next?

WAR BETWEEN the King and the barons continued. But in 1216 John fell ill and died after overeating at a dinner given in his honour.

JOHN'S NINE-YEAR-OLD SON became King Henry III. He wisely made peace with the barons by giving back most of the rights that John had taken from them.

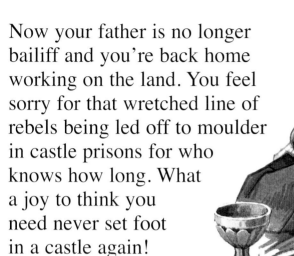

IN 1227 Rochester castle was repaired. The collapsed corner of the keep was given a modern round tower in place of the old square one. Round towers have no corners for the enemy to hide behind.

Glossary* *(Some other important words are explained in the text.)*

Almonry The office where charity was given to the poor.

Anointed king A king who has been crowned in a ceremony which includes blessing with sacred oil.

Armoury A store for armour and weapons.

Bailiff The official in charge of farming on a lord's estate.

Barracks Soldiers' living quarters.

Bolt A short, thick arrow shot from a crossbow.

Brewhouse A place where ale was brewed from malted grain. Ale was safer to drink than untreated water.

Buttery The place where wine and beer were kept, in 'butts' (barrels).

Chamberlain The official in charge of a lord's household arrangements.

Chandlery A place where candles were made.

Constable The commander of a castle.

Damsel A young lady, or a lady-in-waiting.

Dispensary A place where medicines were made.

Distaff A tool for spinning wool to make thread.

Estate The land belonging to a castle.

Farrier An officer who looked after horses.

Great Chamber The second most important room in the keep. It was a more private living space for the lord and his family.

Hall The main room of a keep. Used for official business such as trying criminals and receiving visitors, it was also a communal dining room and sleeping quarters.

Knight A mounted warrior who fought for his lord and was given an estate in return.

Magna Carta A famous legal agreement made in June 1215 between King John and his barons. It removed some power from the king and gave certain rights to the people.

Man-at-arms A highly trained soldier without the status of a knight.

Marshal The official in charge of stabling, hunting and military forces.

Mêlée A fighting contest between groups of knights. A victor kept his opponent's horse – a valuable prize.

Moat A defensive ditch, usually filled with water.

Page A boy of knightly family sent from home to train for knighthood.

Pallet A thin mattress stuffed with straw.

Ransom Money paid for the release of a prisoner. Holding important prisoners to ransom was a normal part of medieval warfare.

Reeve An official elected annually by estate workers to represent their interests with the bailiff and the courts.

Rushes Marsh plants whose long, stiff, grasslike leaves were used as disposable floor coverings.

Scaling ladder A long ladder used by attackers to climb a wall.

Sheriff An officer who enforced the law in a county.

Smithy A blacksmith's workshop.

Squire A youth in the second stage of knightly training, acting as a servant to a knight.

Trencher A slice of stale bread used as a plate, or a wooden plate.

Truckle bed A low bed on wheels, used by a servant. It was put away beneath the master's or mistress's bed.

Villein A peasant entirely subject to his lord, not owning the land he lived on and not allowed to leave it.

Index